NORTHSIDE

SEP 27 2002

D1401770

NS

Transportation & Communication Series

Bridges

Melinda Farbman

Kenosha Public Library
Kenosha, WI

Enslow Publishers, Inc.

40 Industrial Road	PO Box 38
Box 398	Aldershot
Berkeley Heights, NJ 07922	Hants GU12 6BP
USA	UK

http://www.enslow.com

3 0645 7687235

The publisher wishes to thank Laura S. Jeffrey for her efforts in researching and editing this book.

Copyright © 2001 by Enslow Publishers, Inc.

All rights reserved.

No part of this book may be reproduced by any means without the written permission of the publisher.

Library of Congress Cataloging-in-Publication Data

Farbman, Melinda.
   Bridges / Melinda Farbman.
      v. cm. — (Transportation & communication series)
    Includes bibliographical references and index.
    Contents: Bridge Collapse! — Different Kinds of Bridges —
The history of bridges — Names Behind the Bridges — Who builds
bridges?— Bridge to the future.
    ISBN 0-7660-1647-1
    1. Bridges—Juvenile literature.   [1. Bridges.]   I. Title. II. Series.
TG148.F37 2001
621.388'8—dc21   00-011261

Printed in the United States of America

10 9 8 7 6 5 4 3 2 1

To Our Readers: We have done our best to make sure all Internet addresses in this book were active and appropriate when we went to press. However, the author and the publisher have no control over and assume no liability for the material available on those Internet sites or on other Web sites they may link to. Any comments or suggestions can be sent by e-mail to comments@enslow.com or to the address on the back cover.

Every effort has been made to locate all copyright holders of material used in this book. If any errors or omissions have occurred, corrections will be made in future editions of this book.

Illustration Credits: AP Photos/Brian Rasmussen, Nordfoto, p. 36; Corel Corporation, pp. 1, 4, 7, 9, 10, 12, 13, 14, 15, 17, 18 (bottom), 19, 20, 21, 22, 23, 24, 28 (bottom), 30, 32, 34, 35, 38, 40 (top); Dover Publications, Inc., pp. 26 (top), 29 (top); Courtesy of the Frances Loeb Library, Graduate School of Design, Harvard University, p. 27; Hemera Technologies, Inc. 1997–2000, pp. 2, 5, 11, 18 (top), 25, 28 (top), 31, 33, 37, 40 (bottom); Courtesy of Honshu-Shikoku Bridge Authority, p. 39; Hulton Archive, p. 16; Library of Congress, p. 29 (bottom); National Park Service, p. 6 (bottom); Courtesy of the Natural Bridge of Virginia, p. 6 (top); Collections, Rensselaer Polytechnic Institute, Troy, NY 12180, p. 26 (bottom); Beth Townsend, p. 41; Special Collections Division, University of Washington Libraries/ Farguharson, p. 8.

Cover Illustration: Corel Corporation

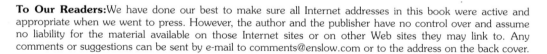

Contents

Chapter 1

Bridge Collapse!

Bridges give people, cars, and trucks a way to cross water, land, and roads. Without bridges, people would need boats to cross rivers. Without bridges, people would have to go around canyons rather than across them.

Some bridges are made by nature. Natural Bridge is in western Virginia. It was formed hundreds of years ago. Water carved a hole into a huge limestone rock. The water carved away the softer rock and left the harder rock. This rock became the bridge. At its widest part, Natural Bridge spans ninety feet. The span of a bridge is the distance between two

Natural bridges are formed by nature (left).

This is the Natural Bridge in western Virginia.

supports. People like to visit and take photos of Natural Bridge.

Agate Bridge is another natural bridge. Agate Bridge is in Petrified Forest National Park in Arizona. Agate Bridge was formed from a tree trunk. It spans forty feet.

Natural Bridge and Agate Bridge were made by nature. But most bridges are made by people. People have built bridges for thousands of years. They use stone, steel, and other strong materials. These bridges must be able to carry a lot of weight. Bridges also need to be strong enough to stand up against tornadoes, hurricanes, and earthquakes. These things can damage or even destroy bridges.

The Tacoma Narrows Bridge was built in 1940. It crossed a river in Bremerton, Washington. The bridge was about a mile

Agate Bridge is in the Petrified Forest National Park in Arizona.

long. At the time, it was the third longest bridge of its kind in the world. People planned the bridge carefully. They made the bridge so it would move with the wind. But the bridge moved too much. It twisted and turned most of the time. People saw the bridge twist and turn even before it was done. They called the bridge "Galloping Gertie." The bridge was finished in the late summer of 1940.

A few months later, on the morning of November 7, 1940, the wind was blowing. The bridge began to move. It twisted and turned for almost an hour. Finally, a support cable snapped. The Tacoma Narrows Bridge collapsed. It crashed into the river. A dog was killed but no people were hurt. People

This is Rainbow Bridge in Arizona.

This is a natural bridge in Bryce Canyon, Colorado.

People could see the Tacoma Narrows Bridge in Washington twist and turn. The bridge fell on November 7, 1940.

tried to find out why the bridge fell down. The disaster taught engineers a lot about planning bridges. They learned that many different things can happen when building a bridge.

In 1951, a new Tacoma Narrows Bridge opened where the old bridge once stood. Today, many cars and trucks go across this bridge. People may build another bridge right next to the old bridge. Or, they may build a new deck below the bridge.

In 1994, an earthquake hit California. Several highway bridges fell down. Many people were killed and hurt. Many millions of dollars were used to build new bridges. The bridges were also made stronger. But until the next earthquake, no one knows for sure if these bridges will stay standing.

Bridges have to be strong enough to stand up to the forces of nature. Here, cement columns support the roadway above.

Chapter 2

Different Kinds of Bridges

Through the years, people have planned different kinds of bridges. They also have tried using different materials. They learned that there are only three basic bridge designs. And there are only a few basic bridge materials.

The three basic bridge designs are beam bridges, arch bridges, and suspension bridges. A beam bridge is the simplest kind of bridge. The roadway, or deck, rests on two piers, one at each end. The piers support the weight of the bridge. They also support any cars and trucks on the bridge. The weight travels downward. If a beam bridge is too long or

People use different materials to build bridges. This bridge (left) is made of wood logs.

Some bridges are not high enough to let big and tall ships go under. Drawbridges can open in the middle to let the ships pass.

holds too much weight, it will sag in the middle and break. Sometimes, supports called trusses are added below the bridge. (Trusses are made of a framework of triangle-shaped metal that makes the bridge stronger.) Beam bridges can span up to 200 feet. Span is the distance between two bridge supports.

Some beam bridges can be moved to let ships pass through. One kind of beam bridge can be lifted up in the middle, like drawbridges. Other kinds of beam bridges are on pivots. They swing sideways to let ships pass.

An arch bridge is shaped like a half of a circle. This shape makes the bridge strong. The arch is strong because of the way it holds weight. As cars and trucks pass over an arch, weight falls downward. It also falls sideways. The arch catches the weight in many different points along its curve: at the top, along the sides, and at the bottom. As weight spreads sideways and downward, it lessens. Arches can span distances of up to 1,000 feet.

Suspension bridges are the third kind of bridge. Cables, ropes, or chains are strung through tall towers. The deck of the bridge hangs, or suspends, from the cables. Suspension bridges usually have trusses underneath. The trusses help to stop the bridge from moving side to side. A suspension bridge looks like a stretched-out "M." It seems

This arch bridge connects two buildings.

The trusses under the roadway of this arch bridge make the bridge stronger.

Hanging bridges are also suspension bridges.

The towers that hold up the cables and the roadway of the bridge are built deep into the water.

to be thin. But it is very strong. Suspension bridges are used when long distances must be crossed. Suspension bridges can span 7,000 feet.

The basic bridge materials are wood, iron, steel, and concrete. Wood was used in the early days because it was easy to find. But wood is not very strong. It bends easily under weight. Wood also rots over time, and it can catch on fire. Iron is stronger than wood. Steel is even stronger than iron. It is often used for long bridges. Concrete is made of cement, sand, gravel, and water.

When concrete hardens, it is hard as rock. Metal is added to concrete to make it stronger.

Strength is important because a bridge has to hold a lot of weight. The weight of traffic moving over a bridge is called live load. Wind, water, heat, and earthquakes are called environmental load. The weight of the bridge itself is called dead load. People think a lot about load when they design bridges.

The cables that hold up the roadway look like they might not be very strong, but they are.

Chapter 3

The History of Bridges

Bridges date back to ancient times. In 537 B.C., a Persian king called Cyrus invented the floating bridge. A roadway lay on top of animal skins. The skins were filled with air and they floated on the water. Another king built a floating military bridge. He tied together two rows of ships. Then, he laid a walkway on top. The bridge was almost a mile long. It took Persian soldiers seven days and seven nights to cross it. They took it apart behind them to get away from their enemy.

The Romans also were very skilled bridge builders. They built many arch bridges of

Old London Bridge (left) was once full of activity in the 1800s. The bridge took thirty-four years to build.

wood and stone. Some are still standing today. The Romans also invented the cofferdam. A cofferdam is an enclosed area used for a short time while building in water. It protects workers from water and cave-ins.

The Romans were very skilled and clever builders as seen here with this bridge (above) and the Colosseum (below).

In the year 1210, the famous Old London Bridge was completed. It was built over the Thames River in London, England. It was lined with buildings, shops, and even a chapel. People gathered on the bridge to walk, shop, and visit friends. Ships stopped to unload goods from other countries. It was a busy place.

Old London Bridge was built of stone. It took thirty-four years to finish. More than 7,000 people drowned or were killed in other accidents while working on the bridge.

Old London Bridge often needed to be fixed. It always seemed to be falling down. New London Bridge was made of concrete. It replaced Old London Bridge in the 1840s. The old bridge was taken apart and shipped to Arizona in the United States. Today, people travel to see it.

In the 1800s, settlers in America built many bridges from wood. These bridges had covers

The Tower of London bridge is a type of drawbridge. The roadway lifts up when a ship needs to pass.

In the 1800s, settlers in America built bridges from wood. Covered bridges not only look pretty, they keep rain, snow, and leaves off of the bridge.

made from wood. The covers protected the bridge from rain and snow. Many of these bridges have been torn down. But in Parke County, Indiana, thirty-two covered bridges still stand. Parke County has more covered bridges than any other place in the world.

The first cast iron arch bridge, the Coalbrookdale Bridge in England, was built in 1779. It weighed 378 tons! The bridge was made of more iron than what was needed. At the time, no one knew how strong iron could be. By the 1800s, people learned that metals are very strong even when a small amount is used.

The Brooklyn Bridge is a steel suspension bridge.

The Brooklyn Bridge in New York City was finished in 1883. It links Brooklyn to the island of Manhattan. The Brooklyn Bridge is a steel suspension bridge. It was the first to be built with steel wire instead of iron wire. There are 75,000 steel wires in each cable. There are four cables. Each cable is more than one foot thick. The towers of the bridge rock slightly. They move with the weight of traffic. Stays, or wires, fan out from the towers. They reach the roadway in crisscrossing triangles of steel. They hold the bridge steady in heavy winds. A promenade, or walkway, stretches across the bridge. People often walk on the promenade between Manhattan and Brooklyn.

On the west coast of the United States is another famous suspension bridge. The Golden Gate Bridge was built in 1937. Its orange, rectangular towers are a symbol of San Francisco, California. The Golden Gate was the first bridge to cross a large ocean harbor. Builders pounded piers into deep,

The Golden Gate Bridge in California, was built in 1937.

open water. San Francisco has many earthquakes. Some earthquakes are so powerful that they can cause the ground to crack and buildings to fall down. To protect the bridge from falling during an earthquake, the bridge foundation was driven 25 feet into bedrock. The Golden Gate Bridge has lasted through many earthquakes.

The Golden Gate Bridge is still standing after many earthquakes.

Chapter 4

Names Behind the Bridges

Thomas Telford was born in Scotland in 1757. He taught himself how to build by helping builders and by reading. Telford was a leader in using iron to build bridges. He built the Menai Straits Bridge in Wales. When it was completed in 1826, it was the longest suspension bridge in the world.

Another important bridge builder was George Stephenson. He was born in England in 1781. At first, Stephenson made shoes and repaired railroad engines for a living. At the age of eighteen, he learned to read and write. Stephenson became an important engineer.

In the early 1880s, these men were working on a railroad bridge (left).

James Eads (above) and John Roebling (below).

George and his son, Robert, made strong railroad bridges in the 1800s.

American James Eads was born in 1820. As a young man, he read math and engineering books. He often searched the Mississippi River for treasure from sunken ships. Later, he used what he had learned about the river to build a railroad bridge in Saint Louis, Missouri.

John Roebling was born in Germany in 1806. He came to live in America, and built a factory in New Jersey. He also built many bridges. In 1869, Roebling had a plan to build the Brooklyn Bridge across the East River in New York City. Many people thought it could not be done. The distance of 1,600 feet seemed too long. Roebling said it would work. But John Roebling never saw the bridge completed. One day in 1869, a ferryboat crushed his foot into a pier. Roebling died of an infection.

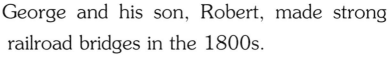

For the next fourteen years, John's son Washington helped build the Brooklyn Bridge. Washington Roebling had studied engineering at Rensselaer Institute in Troy, New York. He fought in the Civil War before taking charge of the bridge project. He worked with others in

The Brooklyn Bridge was finished in 1883.

Today, divers, or people who work underwater, understand the dangers of getting "the bends."

underwater rooms called caissons. Workers entered caissons through underwater stairways called airlocks. Inside the caissons, workers dug mud from the riverbed. As the mud was removed, the caissons sank into deep water. Pressure built up outside. To stop the water pressure from breaking the caissons, workers pumped air into them. The air pressure became higher in the caissons than it was on land.

When a person moves too quickly from high air pressure to low air pressure, nitrogen gas enters the bloodstream. This is called caissons disease, or "the bends." People can become very sick and die. Many workers building the Brooklyn Bridge became sick from "the bends." Washington Roebling was one of them. He became so sick that he had to watch the bridge being built from a bedroom window. Roebling's wife Emily helped him. She became assistant engineer on the project. Every day, Emily carried messages from the Roebling house to the workers at the bridge. Her help moved the project along. In 1883, the Brooklyn Bridge finally opened with fireworks and a parade.

Washington Roebling is pictured above and Emily Roebling is shown below.

Chapter 5

Who Builds Bridges?

Designing and building bridges requires teamwork from many people. Some workers make measurements. They collect information about the number of cars and trucks that cross a bridge each day. This helps to determine the average stress on the bridge. Calculus is the area of math that explains how quantities, or amounts, are always changing. Workers use calculus to find the speed of wind at the place where a bridge might be built. They also use calculus to figure out other forces of nature. Taking all these kinds of measurements help workers figure out how strong the bridge needs to be.

Working together as a team is an important part of any type of project.

Care is taken to make measurements before building begins.

Other workers figure out which materials to use to build a bridge. Workers study chemistry to find out what materials are made of and how they react to air, water, and heat.

Physics is the science that includes the study of motion, light, heat, sound, electricity, and force. Structural engineers study physics to find out how structures move.

Other workers study hydraulics, or the force of water. They need to know how water will affect the bridge supports. They also need to understand how the force of water can change over time.

Some bridge workers know about soil and rocks. They learn that different kinds of soils can take greater weights. This information helps workers figure out where and how bridge supports should be built. Other workers make rules about how wide the lanes should be, and about speed limits. They must apply these rules to the design of the bridge.

Some workers are managers. They make sure every step of the project goes well. Others study new materials and designs. They hope to one day

A lot of planning goes on before building can start.

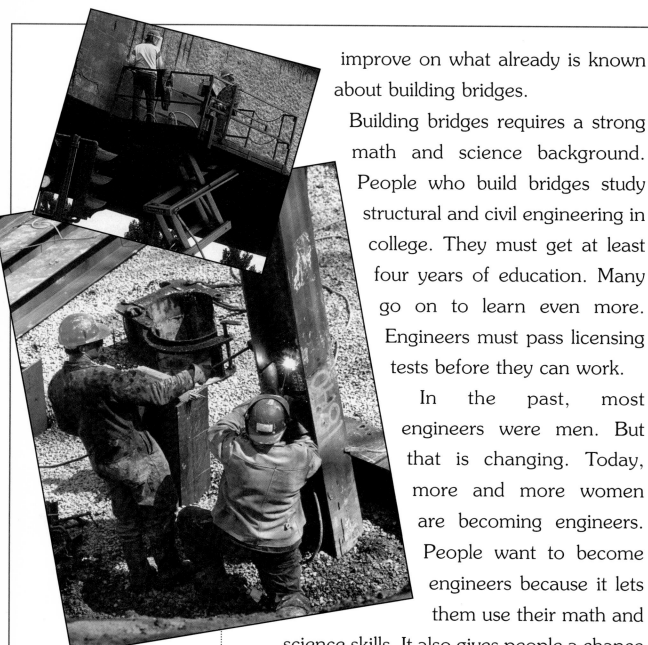

improve on what already is known about building bridges.

Building bridges requires a strong math and science background. People who build bridges study structural and civil engineering in college. They must get at least four years of education. Many go on to learn even more. Engineers must pass licensing tests before they can work.

In the past, most engineers were men. But that is changing. Today, more and more women are becoming engineers. People want to become engineers because it lets them use their math and science skills. It also gives people a chance to build something beautiful and important. People who work well in teams are needed as

People need to work together to get the job done.

engineers. Those with strong computer skills are also needed.

Young people who want to be engineers can get ready by playing with building toys. They can ask engineers questions about the work they do. They can ask math and science teachers to give them problems that have to do with engineering.

The future of engineering is open to anyone who wants to study math and science, use computers, and work with a team to plan and build structures.

Learning how to use a computer is important for people who want to become engineers.

Chapter 6

Bridge to the Future

The Akashi Kaikyo Bridge in Japan may be what bridges in the future will look like. It is the longest suspension bridge in the world. It is over two miles long. It is strong enough to stand up to Japan's heavy rains and earthquakes. Engineers spent twenty years testing plans. Then, they spent ten years building it. The bridge was finished in 1998.

The Oresund Bridge connects Denmark and Sweden. It was finished in July 2000. It is made of concrete and steel. Cars travel on four lanes on the upper deck, or roadway. Trains travel on two tracks on the lower deck. The

The Oresund Bridge (left) connects Denmark and Sweden.

The Akashi Kaikyo Bridge in Japan is over two miles long and is strong enough to withstand Japan's many earthquakes.

This is a cable-stayed bridge.

bridge is a type of suspension bridge called a cable-stayed bridge. On this kind of bridge, cables are strung in a triangle from the towers to the roadway. The towers support the bridge.

Engineers may build a suspension bridge or a tunnel between Sicily and Italy. The island of Sicily is part of Italy. A small body of water separates Sicily and Italy. If a bridge were built, it would span 10,890 feet. The towers would rise to 1,312 feet. The bridge would hold both a twelve-lane highway and a railroad track.

Many engineers have tried to design a

Lakeshore Bridge in Chicago, Illinois.

bridge to cross the Gibraltar Strait. This small body of water is between Spain and Morocco. Spain is a country in Europe. Morocco is a country in Africa. One idea is to build a nine-mile bridge on top of two columns. Another idea is to build piers on top of pontoons. Pontoons are flat-bottomed boats. The pontoons would be anchored to the ocean floor with cables.

In 1958, engineer T.Y. Lin shared his plan for the Inter-Continental Peace Bridge. It was for a bridge between Alaska and Siberia. Lin's bridge would be a symbol of peace between

Building a bridge in these sort of conditions can be tricky.

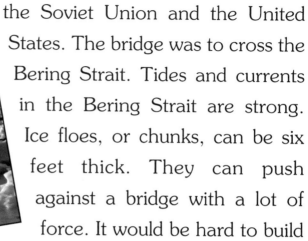

the Soviet Union and the United States. The bridge was to cross the Bering Strait. Tides and currents in the Bering Strait are strong. Ice floes, or chunks, can be six feet thick. They can push against a bridge with a lot of force. It would be hard to build a long bridge in cold, icy conditions. Since Lin planned the bridge, the Soviet Union fell. The United States and Russia are at peace. Plans to build the bridge are on hold.

Yet one day, that bridge and many others may be built. Since ancient times, people have built bridges. Rocks and tree trunks gave way to steel, iron, and concrete. In the future, glass and plastic may also be used. These materials are lighter than metal. They also last longer.

Bridges provide links from one point to another. In the future, they may be able to cross even longer distances. Who knows? One day, bridges may connect continents.

Types of Bridges

Arch

Beam

Cable-Stayed

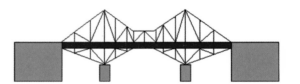

Cantilever

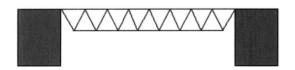

Deck Truss

Suspension

The Longest Bridges

Type	Name	Place	Span (in feet)	Year Completed
Steel Arch	New River George	West Virginia, USA	1,700	1977
	Bayonne	New Jersey, USA	1,652	1931
	Sydney Harbour	Australia	1,650	1932
	Zdakov	Czech Republic	1,256	1967
Suspension	Akashi Kaikyo	Japan	6,570	1998
	Storebaelt	Denmark	5,328	1998
	Humber	England	4,626	1981
	Jiangyin Yangtze	China	4,544	1999
Cable-Stayed	Tatara	Japan	2,920	1999
	Pont de Normandie	France	2,808	1995
	Quingzhou Minjang	China	1,985	1996
	Yangpu	China	1,975	1993
Cantilever	Quebec Bridge	Canada	1,800	1917
	Forth	Scotland	1,710	1917
	Nanko	Japan	1,673	1974
	Commodore John Barry Bridge	New Jersey/ Pennsylvania, USA	1,644	1974

Timeline

537 B.C.—Persian king Cyrus invents the floating bridge.

300 B.C.–A.D. 300—Romans invent the cofferdam.

1210—First London Bridge is finished.

1779—Coalbrookdale Bridge is the first cast iron arch bridge.

1874—James Eads builds the first steel bridge in St. Louis, Missouri.

1883—Brooklyn Bridge opens.

1937—Golden Gate Bridge in San Francisco, California, is the first bridge to cross a large ocean harbor.

1940—42-mile per hour winds cause the Tacoma Narrows Bridge in Washington to fall.

1998—Akashi Kaikyo Bridge in Japan is the longest suspension bridge.

2000—Oresund Bridge connects Denmark and Sweden.

Words to Know

arch—A curved structure used as a support over an open space.

beam—A long, thick piece of wood, metal, or stone used in building.

bedrock—Solid rock under the soil.

cable—A thick, heavy rope made of wire.

cantilever—A beam that goes past its support.

chemistry—The science that deals with substances, what they are made of, what characteristics they have, and what kinds of changes happen when they combine with other substances.

earthquake—A shaking or trembling of the ground. An earthquake is caused by rock, lava, or hot gases moving deep inside the earth.

Words to Know

engineering—The work that uses scientific knowledge for practical things, such as building bridges and dams.

physics—The science that deals with matter and energy and the laws governing them.

pier—A strong structure supporting the spans of a bridge.

span—The part of a bridge that is between two supports.

suspension bridge—A bridge suspended by cables anchored at both ends and supported by towers.

trusses—A framework of triangle-shaped metal. Trusses do not move when force is pushed down on them. This makes them very strong.

Learn More About
Bridges

Books

Johnmann, Carol A. and Elizabeth J. Reith. *Bridges!: Amazing Structures to Design, Build & Test.* Charlotte, Vt.: Williamson Publishing Co, 1999.

Kaner, Etta. *Bridges.* Buffalo, N.Y.: Kids Can Press Ltd., 1994.

Oxlade, Chris. *Bridges.* Chicago, Ill.: Heinemann Library, 2000.

Pollard, Michael. *Amazing Structures.* New York, N.Y.: Barnes & Noble Books, 1996.

Ricciuti, Edward R. *America's Top 10 Bridges.* Woodbridge, Conn.: Blackbirch Press, 1997.

Learn More About
Bridges

Internet Addresses

How Stuff Works: How Bridges Work

<http://www.howstuffworks.com/bridge.htm>

This site has pictures and photos that talk about different types of bridges.

NOVA Online: Super Bridge

<http://www.pbs.org/wgbh/nova/bridge/>

Click on "Build a Bridge" to figure out which type of bridge goes where.

The Great Buildings Online: Brooklyn Bridge

<http://www.greatbuildings.com/buildings/ Brooklyn_Bridge.html>

Get some quick facts about the Brooklyn Bridge. Search for other bridges and people who built the bridges.

Index